Also By George Held

The Art of Writing and Others (Finishing Line Press, 2007)

W Is for War (Červená Barva Press, 2006)

Martial Artist (Toad Press, 2005), translator

Grounded (Finishing Line Press, 2005)

Untitled e-book at www.thehypertexts.com (2004)

American Poetry (The New Formalist Press, 2003)

Touched by Eros (The Live Poets Society, 2002), editor

Beyond Renewal (Cedar Hill, 2001)

Absolut Death and Others, with paintings by Roz Dimon (Dimon Studios, 2000)

Open and Shut (Talent House Press, 1999)

Salamander Love and Others (Talent House Press, 1998)

Winged (Birnam Wood, 1995)

PHASED

Poems, etc.

by

George Held

POETS WEAR PRADA • Hoboken, New Jersey

Phased

First North American Publication 2008.

http://pwpbooks.blogspot.com/

Grateful acknowledgment is made to the following publications, in which these poems, sometimes in different form, have appeared:

The Aurorean, Best Poem, Brevities, Connecticut Review, The Dark of the Moon, Home Planet News, Libido, Long Island Sounds: 2007 (The North Sea Poetry Scene Press), *The Moon, Miller's Pond, Off the Coast, Persimmon, Piedmont Literary Review, Point Judith Light, Potpourri, Raw NerVZ Haiku, Salamander Love and Others* (Talent House Press), *W Is for War* (Červená Barva Press), *Waterways*, and *Whole Notes*.

ISBN 978-0-9817678-0-2

Printed in the U.S.A.

Front Cover: Jean Held
Back Cover Author Photo: Jean Held
Illustration on the Final Page: George Held

Contents

For Webb and Marguerite, Jamison and Haydn

Sara and Norman and Tyler

Roz and James

Cheryl

Phased

Ghostly, in a shroud
Of early morning cloud,

The last-quarter moon
Accents the day's gloom

Phasing down to new,
When I'll have no view

Of even a crescent
For a night or two

Until the first quarter
Reveals its presence.

Then I'll be back in phase
With its monthly cycle,

Pulled like a woman
Toward her period,

An ineffable force
That's far from a curse,

That leaves me phased,
On the cusp of pleased.

Call of the Wolf

The full wolf moon marked January's dearth,
when hunger shrank our guts and brought the wolf
to our village. We hunted and foraged
by day; by night, when the campfires had sunk,
we huddled in our blankets, bodies spooned
with mate or comrade, wakeful to the howls
nearby. The wolves hungered for our victuals
tied in bundles to the boughs above us
or for our babies bundled beside us.
Few deer remained for man or wolf to hunt;
Pemmican gone, squirrel, 'possum, or vole,
roots and dried berries our diet. The old
suffered most from the cold, and some abstained
from eating; most uncomplainingly bowed
to scarcity that the young and fit might live.
But not my father. An old sachem, he
insisted on his ration yet couldn't help
find provisions, his lameness, like a hawk's
broken wing, dooming him to starve, to die.
Yet he demanded food; no squalling babe
sought teat more clamorously than he howled
for morsel from the spit, the smell of meat
making his gut twinge, maddening him so
he lost his bearing, became a disgrace

to himself and to me. I did not need
to see my comrades scowl or hear them growl.
I knew what I must do. And so I bound
my howling father to a sled when day
broke and snow fell to obscure the full wolf
moon as it set. I tied the harness round
my waist and entered the woods, dragging its
cargo along the trail newly covered
with snow. If my father moaned, my panting
drowned out the sound. I heard just my feet crunch
the snow, twigs snap, the shush of sled behind.
Five leagues I labored till I reached Rook Hill,
then stopped at the appointed place. Other
sons had long brought their aged fathers there,
and my own son might bring me unless Fate
deemed I die in battle or have the will
to walk, while still I can, into the woods
to die. As I lift Father from the sled
and lay him on the snow, so resolute
he looks that joy dispels all sorrow from
my heart. The snow has stopped. "This is farewell,
old man. You have served your people well; now
they starve till spring returns. In spring we shall
renew ourselves and we shall honor your deeds."
"My son, I pray these last querulous months
have not defamed my honor, my spirit.
On our journey, as I lay behind you,
I could resign myself to Fate. You have
always done right by me, never more so

than now." "My father, you have also now
done right, and I shall leave you with this blade.
Use it as you desire, or not," I say
as I hand him my hunting knife. I rise
and take the sled's harness in hand, then turn
back to the trail. Barely a league I walk
when on the still air comes the first wolf call,
Fate's call. Soon a chorus of calls drifts
through the woods, and I picture my father
driving wolves away from the bear he'd killed
till his comrades came to help him drag it
home, where bear steaks fed us and a bear coat
kept me warm. I draw it tight and walk toward home.

The Full Snow Moon

Why have I all but forgotten you,
The moon that lights the frozen waste
Of white that covers ground
In our neck of the woods—

Because for years there was no snow
In February, because now there is too much
To treasure, just a seasonal annoyance
That hems us into the woods?

Oh, yes, I feel your pull and revel
In your glow, like a crystal ball
Telling that the future is snowmelt,
Ice fracture, floods of March.

So you still signify, still highlight
Not the depths but the end of winter,
Snow man, old man, high-falutin' man
Floating above the woods.

Names for the March Full Moon

I. The Full Worm Moon

Days grow milder,
worm casts rising from thawed earth—
robins soon

II. The Full Crow Moon

Days grow milder,
north-woods crows cawing loud—
the smell of skunk cabbage

III. The Full Crust Moon

Days grow milder,
melting snow, freezing crust at night—
the scent of witch hazel

IV. The Full Sap Moon

Days grow milder,
maple sap runs, tap dripping—
ah, the sweetness

Afternoon Moon

4:45 PM, walking Job's Lane, Southampton,
azure sky after two days of April rain,
temperature rising, spring finally springing,
and high above the redbudded maple tops
the silver three-quarter moon,
almost transparent, steals the scene
from The Driver's Seat and the Parrish Museum
and the sidewalks crowded with window shoppers,
and I think of Frank O'Hara and Fairfield Porter
and the other stars of the cultural firmament
who also strolled this street, heads springing
ideas for poems or paintings
and for whom the late-afternoon moon
had to be just as corny an inspiration
as for me.

The Full Pink Moon

April's full moon gets its name from the herb moss pink, which is one of the earliest widespread flowers of spring.

O Moon, you're about the right distance
From Earth, far enough to avoid the stinks
And turmoils but too far to smell the flowers
Or see their yellows, reds, and pinks

Or witness Earthlings' occasional kindness
And not too far to view a nuclear holocaust
Or a sand storm in the growing desert
If it's on the side that's facing you.

How I love to see your bland face
Rising above it all, like a discus
Or Communion wafer or sign of God's
Indifference or maybe of His

Or Her distant benevolence,
If the pious even notice
You. Just stay where you are,
Hanging out up there in the black,

So blank yet so mimetic,
So void yet so iconic.

...And Cream

(For Cheryl)

June's full moon gets its name from the strawberry harvest that
happens every year at this time.

That lemon lozenge dissolving the night
In strawberry season gives pause
For thoughts about shortcake and cream,
Vanilla ice cream, or Cheerios topped with red
Fruit, about strawberry blondes like Basinger,
Darryl the Mets' monster slugger, whom some fans
Cheered and others gave the raspberry.

Ever notice that the smaller strawberry tastes
Authentic, while the humongous ones grown to ship
Where berries are out of season have no flavor,
Aroma, or lush texture? Who ever tastes
A strawberry today like the ones we picked
In the 'Fifties, sucking our red fingers
Like a piece of sugar cane? Fruit then
Was seasonal—tomatoes from July
Through September, apples from then
Till December. Remember how they tasted
Edenically true?

Today's gassed, synthetically
Colored facsimiles remind us of our fallen
State. Even the moon bears garbage,
But the old full moon still tastes sweet
Dissolving the old night over the old
Strawberry fields, forever.

Honey Moon

At ten the white-pine tops are backlighted
By an orange glow that stops me in mid-
Stride. Soon the red disc of the Honey Moon
Follows its aureole over the trees,
And I'm tempted to rhyme "moon" with "June," but
Such custom betrays the unaccustomed
Glory of this celestial sight. One night
A year this lowest of all the full moons
On the horizon gilds the east. I might
Have been at the movies, or cloud-cover
Could have obscured this weird phenomenon.
From now on, for however many moons
I'll be around, I'll free my calendar
To let me keep this moon-struck rendezvous.

Looking at the Moon

Racing with the moon,
High above the midnight gloom...

Blue Moon, you saw me standing alone...

I was looking at the Red, or Sturgeon, moon the other night and thinking that the culture has come a long way in its regard for the moon since those song lyrics were popular in the 1940s. The first moon landing, in 1969, now 37 years ago, taught us what the moon's surface looks like. We're aware that some earth litter has been left there. We've seen that Saturn's moons, beautifully photographed by satellite in 2004, are more varied and enigmatic than ours. So our moon—The Moon—seems both closer than about 240,000 miles from Earth and less mysterious than it ever has to us Earthlings.

Fly me to the moon...

Some might say we are better off with the moon demystified, that it's better to understand it as an astrophysical object than as a source of earthly superstition—better to know its substance consists of minerals and rocks related to its sister, Earth, than of green cheese. Better that the Man in the Moon doesn't live there anymore. Better that no cow jumps over the moon.

My mother taught me that the moon's magnetic pull became so strong at full moon that it turned some folks into lunatics. Apparently, there is some evidence that murders and vampirism peak during the night of a full moon. For decades I awoke after midnight when the moon was full and got up to look at it from my window. Its brightness left me too spellbound to get back to sleep till dawn. I was, as I came to think of it, moonstruck.

I look at you and suddenly,
Something in your eyes I see,
Soon begins bewitching me,
It's that Old Devil Moon...

In school I learned that in Roman mythology Diana the huntress, that supreme athlete and symbol of chastity, was a moon goddess. The moon thus registers Diana's coolness, aloofness, and distance from earthbound men. My favorite two things associated with Diana are that slaves could find asylum in her temple and that modern Freemasons believe she symbolizes the imagination and the creative lunacy of artists and poets.

When I first studied foreign languages, I was keen to learn the word for "moon": "luna" in Latin, and thus also in Italian and Spanish, "lune" in French, contained the root for "lunatic." Old English "mona," cognate with German "Mond," gave us Monday ("lundi" in French).

I see a pale moon arisin'...

When I began to write poems, the moon was an obvious subject. I've published about two-dozen moon poems and have others unpublished. But I confess the moon still inspires and interests me for its influence—the inflowing of its light and lore—more than for its physical properties. Though I now sometimes sleep all night when the moon is full, I still admire its beauty as it goes through its monthly phases.

In August 2005 I attended a minor league baseball game in Oneonta, in upstate New York. A local bank had provided free tickets as part of a promotion, and the seats were full of fans, from two to 92. The game was exciting, young men going all-out for a shot at the Bigs, though the home team Tigers languished behind until their last at-bat, when they rallied to beat the Staten Island Yankees, 10-9.

All the while I sat on the bleacher plank I was aware that a crescent moon was pasted in the sky above right field. At first barely noticeable in the sun's last rays, about 40 degrees above the horizon, the new moon and the evening star helped provide a backdrop for the Norman Rockwell scene at the ballpark. By 10:30, when the game ended, the now bright crescent rested upon the treetops, its setting synchronized with the conclusion of the game and the emptying of the seats.

The dark of the moon occurs when the moon is "new," the waning crescent having disappeared and the new crescent having yet to materialize. "Once in a blue moon" refers to the so-called thirteenth moon in any year, when one month has two full moons, about 29 days apart, or when four full moons occur in any of the four seasons. The thirteenth moon is also associated with menopause, and a feminist literary magazine is called *13th Moon*.

What value does such consciousness of our satellite have? It's arguably just a way of continuing an age-old tradition of honoring, even worshipping, the moon and acknowledging our presence in the natural world and the larger universe. Especially in New York City, where I live, it's well to look for the moon as it goes through its phases, like the family dog doing its tricks. We've seen them before and will have a chance to see them again, but the moon—quarter, half, full—tells us that tonight, right now, is what counts: Look at me, it says, in the present, feel my pull, imagine my power, don't be merely an Earthling but also be a Lunatic.

Moonglow

The way the moon
   Shone down on me
A gleam of light
   From its apogee

Has given me a glimpse
   Of ecstasy,
The benefit
   Of lunacy.

To Moon

Though you've been praised for millenniums,
I still am drawn to you phase by phase;
You're Earth's celestial sister, reflector
Of Sun's light, rarely eclipsed, about whom
There's not much new to say, but please just stay
Up there and pull the tides. When you rise over
Long Island potato fields, your glow
Enchants the land and me; your karma charms
Lovers and alarms lunatics, we know,
But even if you had no pull, you'd please
Most with your beauty as you pass from slim
Crescent to full of yourself in four weeks,
Then leave us in the dark of the new you.
O Moon, I'm such a sucker, stuck on you!

Anti-romantic Moon

The Hay Moon shone like a klieg light
through a black scrim—bright
and shiny as a celestial coin,
every continent of the realm
clear as in an Apollo photo.

Our eyes blinked back its intensity
but it compelled us to look
until tears made us avert
our gaze and we fixed
our stares on each other's eyes

and felt a tidal tug. That moon's shrill light
ruled out romance but roused
a phase of genital desire.
Our lips ripped each other,
Our hands groped for what we hoped

was paydirt. As I wriggled my finger
inside your panties, you unearthed me
and we brought each other off there
by the roadside in the metallic glare
of that anti-romantic full moon.

Moon Haiku

Midnight full moon
pulling me from bed
　　into its orbit

Manhattan lights
seen from Hoboken—
　　the half moon

The Flower Moon
shining upon the lane—
　　horse chestnuts bloom

November moonlight—
the hoarfrost glistening
　　on the lawn

Harvest moon silvers
St. Vincent's Hospital—
　　silent the AIDS ward

Working Girl Eyes the Moon

After leaving her SoHo office at nine,
She crosses Sixth and heads uptown toward home
When the brazen full moon catches her eye
And whistles at her.

She smiles and eyes the moon, that old devil,
Who wants her to look while he moons her,
Hoping to drive her loony, or luny—
O clair de la lune.

And she's just tired enough to fall for him,
The man in the, that big cheese in the East,
But she just absorbs his aura, his moonshine,
That shows her the way to go home.

The Hunter's Moon

The Hunter's Moon is the first full moon following the Harvest Moon, which is the closest full moon to the Autumnal Equinox.
— American Indian calendar

Flooding the October sky
You sent the Mohawks
On the deer path, kept the Hurons
From the warpath until
The new moon, the stealthy
Warrior's eyes taking advantage
Of the dark, the hunter
Willing his prey to make its meat
A gift to the spirit
Of the archer.

Now you watch the modern Hurons
Engage in war
So mechanized no sachem
Would countenance it:
Desert warriors in hi-tech suits sight
Through electronic lenses
And launch unerring lasers;
The prey are harvested
And stacked like logs
In the moonlight.

Cataract Moon

That Full Cold Moon wears an aureole
It never had before, a rainbow of blurred light
Around its rim.

As I await my cataractectomy, snow men
And refrigerators yellow, and night deepens
To make me blind.

My blurred vision sets me in a sci-fi world,
Where mutation is the rule, ontological insecurity
Seems palpable.

Driving at night became too adventurous
Once oncoming headlights glared halos
That blinded me.

Reading, my lifelong mistress, now vexes me
As letters fade and words melt like a watch
Tanguy painted.

Greek *katarraktes* suggests a waterfall flowing
before my only sighted eye, a portcullis lowered
On my vision.

How much can I expect to see
Through such closed blinds, how long till,
Cataract ripe,

It can be emulsified and vacuumed out,
Then replaced with a clear prosthetic lens,
Restoring sight?

Or will this blurry orb be the last full moon
I'll ever see should surgery fail
To restore sight?

Or, sight restored, this yellow page white again,
Will I miss the mysterious world my cataract
Now affords me?

Waning

I raise the blind at dawn, ten degrees
Out there, and I see the half moon
Low in the cobalt southwest,

The day waxing and the moon waning,
Like my life, like my arrhythmic heart.
How many more cycles to fullness

Will I see that old moon achieve,
That lifetime partner in isolation,
Basking in mute reflected glory

While wearing the ball and chain,
Sentenced to wax and wane
Up there while few necks crane

To admire her or him or it—Diana,
The Old Man, that geologic target
Of telescope and spaceman.

The sky lightens to pale blue
Blanching the moon's hue.
Why would anyone turn on the tube

While this light show's going on?
But there's work to be done and one
Can hardly spend hours watching

The moon wane, slim day by day
To a sliver, then wax new again
In a way that humans never can.

Inebriates' Delight

The full moon a bung-hole,
Pouring vintage to earth;
We drink it down in verse
And song, refreshing soul.

Acknowledgments

Grateful acknowledgment is made to the following publications, in which these poems, sometimes in different form, have appeared:

"Phased"	*Best Poem*
"Names for the March Full Moon"	*The Aurorean*
"Afternoon Moon"	*Connecticut Review*
"The Full Pink Moon"	*Off the Coast*
"... And Cream"	*Waterways*
"Honey Moon"	*Whole Notes*
"Looking at the Moon"	*The Dark of the Moon*
"Moonglow"	*Brevities*
"To Moon"	*The Moon*
"Anti-romantic Moon"	*Libido*
"Moon Haiku":	
"The Flower Moon"	*Persimmon*
"Midnight Full Moon"	*Piedmont Literary Review*
"November Moonlight"	*Point Judith Light*
"Moonlight on Roadside"	*Potpourri*
"Harvest Moon Silvers"	*Raw NerVZ Haiku*
"The Hunter's Moon"	*Home Planet News*
"Cataract Moon"	*Miller's Pond*

"Afternoon Moon" also appeared in the anthology *Long Island Sounds: 2007* (The North Sea Poetry Scene Press, 2007). "Anti-romantic Moon" was previously published in *Salamander Love and Others* (Talent House Press, 1998), and "The Hunter's Moon" appeared in *W Is for War* (Červená Barva Press, 2006).

About the Author

George Held is the author of 14 poetry collections and the editor of the anthology *Touched by Eros*. A five-time nominee for the Pushcart Prize, he has published his stories, poems, book reviews, and translations in such places as *The Philadelphia Inquirer*, *Circumfere*nce, *The Notre Dame Review*, *Commonweal*, *Connecticut Review*, and *Confrontation*. His most recent book is *After Shakespeare: Selected Sonnets* (Červená Barva Press, 2010). In December 2007, his poem "Aftermath" was read by Garrison Keillor on *The Writer's Almanac*. He has co-edited *The Ledge Poetry and Fiction Magazine* since 1991, the same year he joined the executive board of The South Fork Natural History Society and Museum (Bridgehampton, NY). A Fulbright lecturer in Czechoslovakia 1973-76, he retired as a professor of English at Queens College in 2004. Held resides in Greenwich Village with his wife, Cheryl.

www.ingramcontent.com/pod-product-compliance
Lightning Source LLC
Chambersburg PA
CBHW061759040426
42447CB00011B/2379